1 MONTH OF
FREE
READING

at

www.ForgottenBooks.com

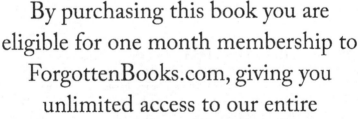

By purchasing this book you are eligible for one month membership to ForgottenBooks.com, giving you unlimited access to our entire collection of over 700,000 titles via our web site and mobile apps.

To claim your free month visit:

www.forgottenbooks.com/free554535

ISBN 978-0-484-23921-9
PIBN 10554535

COMMUNIST ESPIONAGE IN THE UNITED STATES
TESTIMONY OF FRANTISEK TISLER
Former Military and Air Attaché, Czechoslovak Embassy in Washington, D.C.

HEARING

BEFORE THE

COMMITTEE ON UN-AMERICAN ACTIVITIES
HOUSE OF REPRESENTATIVES

EIGHTY-SIXTH CONGRESS
SECOND SESSION

RELEASED MAY 10, 1960

Printed for the use of the Committee on Un-American Activities

INCLUDING INDEX

UNITED STATES
GOVERNMENT PRINTING OFFICE
54527°   WASHINGTON : 1960

COMMITTEE ON UN-AMERICAN ACTIVITIES
UNITED STATES HOUSE OF REPRESENTATIVES

FRANCIS E. WALTER, Pennsylvania, *Chairman*

MORGAN M. MOULDER, Missouri
CLYDE DOYLE, California
EDWIN E. WILLIS, Louisiana
WILLIAM M. TUCK, Virginia

DONALD L. JACKSON, California
GORDON H. SCHERER, Ohio
WILLIAM E. MILLER, New York
AUGUST E. JOHANSEN, Michigan

RICHARD ARENS, *Staff Director*

II

CONTENTS

III

The legislation under which the House Committee on Un-American Activities operates is Public Law 601, 79th Congress [1946], chapter 753, 2d session, which provides:

Be it enacted by the Senate and House of Representatives of the United States of America in Congress assembled, * * *

PART 2—RULES OF THE HOUSE OF REPRESENTATIVES

RULE X

SEC. 121. STANDING COMMITTEES

    *   *   *   *   *   *   *

17. Committee on Un-American Activities, to consist of nine Members.

RULE XI

POWERS AND DUTIES OF COMMITTEES

    *   *   *   *   *

(q) (1) Committee on Un-American Activities.

(A) Un-American activities.

(2) The Committee on Un-American Activities, as a whole or by subcommittee, is authorized to make from time to time investigations of (i) the extent, character, and objects of un-American propaganda activities in the United States, (ii) the diffusion within the United States of subversive and un-American propaganda that is instigated from foreign countries or of a domestic origin and attacks the principle of the form of government as guaranteed by our Constitution, and (iii) all other questions in relation thereto that would aid Congress in any necessary remedial legislation.

The Committee on Un-American Activities shall report to the House (or to the Clerk of the House if the House is not in session) the results of any such investigation, together with such recommendations as it deems advisable.

For the purpose of any such investigation, the Committee on Un-American Activities, or any subcommittee thereof, is authorized to sit and act at such times and places within the United States, whether or not the House is sitting, has recessed, or has adjourned, to hold such hearings, to require the attendance of such witnesses and the production of such books, papers, and documents, and to take such testimony, as it deems necessary. Subpenas may be issued under the signature of the chairman of the committee or any subcommittee, or by any member designated by any such chairman, and may be served by any person designated by any such chairman or member.

    *   *   *   *   *   *   *

RULE XII

LEGISLATIVE OVERSIGHT BY STANDING COMMITTEES

SEC. 136. To assist the Congress in appraising the administration of the laws and in developing such amendments or related legislation as it may deem necessary, each standing committee of the Senate and the House of Representatives shall exercise continuous watchfulness of the execution by the administrative agencies concerned of any laws, the subject matter of which is within the jurisdiction of such committee; and, for that purpose, shall study all pertinent reports and data submitted to the Congress by the agencies in the executive branch of the Government.

RULES ADOPTED BY THE 86TH CONGRESS

House Resolution 7, January 7, 1959

*   *   *   *

RULE X

STANDING COMMITTEES

1. There shall be elected by the House, at the commencement of each Con-gress,

*   *   *   *   *   *   *

(q) Committee on Un-American Activities, to consist of nine Members.

*   *   *   *   *   *   *

RULE XI

POWERS AND DUTIES OF COMMITTEES

*   *   *   *   *

18. Committee on Un-American Activities.
(a) Un-American activities.
(b) The Committee on Un-American Activities, as a whole or by subcommittee, is authorized to make from time to time investigations of (1) the extent, char-acter, and objects of un-American propaganda activities in the United States, (2) the diffusion within the United States of subversive and un-American prop-aganda that is instigated from foreign countries or of a domestic origin and attacks the principle of the form of government as guaranteed by our Constitu-tion, and (3) all other questions in relation thereto that would aid Congress in any necessary remedial legislation.

The Committee on Un-American Activities shall report to the House (or to the Clerk of the House if the House is not in session) the results of any such investi-gation, together with such recommendations as it deems advisable.

For the purpose of any such investigation, the Committee on Un-American Activities, or any subcommittee thereof, is authorized to sit and act at such times and places within the United States, whether or not the House is sitting, has recessed, or has adjourned, to hold such hearings, to require the attendance of such witnesses and the production of such books, papers, and documents, and to take such testimony, as it deems necessary. Subpenas may be issued under the signature of the chairman of the committee or any subcommittee, or by any member designated by any such chairman, and may be served by any person designated by any such chairman or member.

*   *   *   *   *   *   *

26. To assist the House in appraising the administration of the laws and in developing such amendments or related legislation as it may deem necessary, each standing committee of the House shall exercise continuous watchfulness of the execution by the administrative agencies concerned of any laws, the subject matter of which is within the jurisdiction of such committee; and, for that purpose, shall study all pertinent reports and data submitted to the House by the agencies in the executive branch of the Government.

COMMUNIST ESPIONAGE IN THE UNITED STATES

Testimony of Frantisek Tisler, Former Military and Air Attaché, Czechoslovak Embassy in Washington, D. C.

UNITED STATES HOUSE OF REPRESENTATIVES,
COMMITTEE ON UN-AMERICAN ACTIVITIES,
Washington, D.C.

The committee met in executive session pursuant to call, Honorable Francis E. Walter, chairman, presiding.

Committee members present: Representatives Francis E. Walter of Pennsylvania and Gordon H. Scherer of Ohio.

Staff members present: Richard Arens, staff director, and Donald T. Appell, investigator.

The CHAIRMAN. May we come to order.

Will you raise your right hand, please? Do you swear the testimony you are about to give in the matter now pending will be the truth, the whole truth, and nothing but the truth, so help you God?

Mr. TISLER. I do.

TESTIMONY OF FRANTISEK TISLER, FORMER MILITARY AND AIR ATTACHÉ, CZECHOSLOVAK EMBASSY, WASHINGTON, D.C.

The CHAIRMAN. Let the record show that this particular hearing is being held at a time and place which cannot be revealed on the record.

Proceed, Mr. Arens.

Mr. ARENS. Kindly identify yourself by name, date and place of birth, and previous occupational specialty.

Mr. TISLER. I am Frantisek Tisler and I was born on the 13th of December 1924 in Temelin, Czechoslovakia. Temelin is located in the district of Tyn nad Vltavou in southern Bohemia, and at the time of my youth this was a rural agricultural area. Prior to the 25th of July 1959 my last position was that of Military and Air Attaché at the Czechoslovak Embassy in Washington, D.C. As a result of my overt duties as military and air attaché, I held the rank of lieutenant colonel in the Czechoslovak Army. In addition to my duties as military and air attaché, I was the chief of the Czechoslovak Military Intelligence Directorate Residentura, which had its headquarters at the Czechoslovak Embassy in Washington, D.C., from which I defected in July 1959.

Mr. ARENS. Off the record.

(Discussion off the record.)

Mr. ARENS. In other words, Colonel Tisler, you were both a professional army officer and an intelligence officer prior to the time of your defection?

Mr. TISLER. Yes, that is correct.

Mr. ARENS. Would you please furnish us with a synopsis of your educational background?

Mr. TISLER. I attended an elementary school for 5 years in Temelin and then entered the Jursikovo Gymnasium in Ceske Budejovice. After 1938 I continued my gymnasium education at the Jiraskovo Gymnasium in Prague. I obtained a matura from this gymnasium in 1943. After I obtained my matura I attempted to enter a number of commercial art schools but was unable to do so, as a result of a law which the German occupation forces in Czechoslovakia had issued and which stated that no individual who was born in 1924 could continue schooling beyond the matura level.

This directive by the Germans decreed that all such individuals must work rather than attend school. As a result, my education was interrupted until July 1945. I entered the commercial college (Vysoka Skola Obchodni) in Prague in July 1945, but in view of financial difficulties as well as the extremely crowded conditions which prevailed at this school at that time, I was forced to discontinue attendance. In October 1945, I was admitted to the philosophic faculty of Charles University in Prague. I studied at Charles University until 1947, but finally withdrew from the university prior to the beginning of the fall semester of 1947, due to financial and family considerations.

When I did not return to Charles University for the fall semester, I was subsequently drafted into the Czechoslovak Army on October 1, 1947. In November 1947 I was assigned to a reserve officers' school at Klatovy, and I stayed at this school until May 1948. In October 1948 I entered the regular infantry officers' school at Hranice, and I subsequently graduated from this school in August 1949, with the rank of 2d lieutenant. At the time that I attended this school, it was known as the Military Academy (Vojenska Akademie). In October 1951 I started to attend the Military Staff School (Vojenska Akademie Klementa Gottvalda) located in Prague. I graduated from this Military Staff School in July 1954, and this represented the completion of my formal training as an army officer. I subsequently received additional training but this was specialized training for my activities as a military intelligence officer.

Mr. ARENS. If you don't mind, Colonel Tisler, we would prefer to return to your training as a military intelligence officer at a later portion of this session.

Mr. TISLER. I understand.

Mr. ARENS. It would be appreciated if you would outline briefly your family background.

Mr. TISLER. My father is still residing in Czechoslovakia, and he is retired due to a bone disease and serious heart condition. My father was a tailor by profession. My mother is also living in Czechoslovakia at the present time, and she is a maternity nurse by profession, although to the best of my knowledge she is no longer working, because she has to spend most of her time taking care of my father. I have a brother who is also residing in Czechoslovakia at the present time, but he too suffers from a physical disability which he obtained as a result of working in the northern Bohemian coal mines. He is also retired. I have a sister who is also in Czechoslovakia and, as far as I know, she is employed in the Ministry of Internal Trade.

Mr. ARENS. Would you mind telling us, Colonel, if you are married and if you have any children?

Mr. TISLER. Yes, I am married and my wife, Adela Tisler, nee Machacek, born March 27, 1926, at Jihlava, is a well-known amateur athlete. In the years 1947, 1948, 1954, and 1955 she was the women's champion of Czechoslovakia in the shotput. In 1956 my wife was awarded the title Master of Sport by the Czechoslovak Government. We have been fortunate enough to have children, and these children are with us in the United States.

Mr. ARENS. Please give us a brief synopsis of your wartime activities at the time that Czechoslovakia was under German occupation.

Mr. TISLER. As of September 1943 I was assigned by the labor office to work at the Czech Moravian Machine Company in Prague, Holesovice. After this I was assigned to forced labor tasks in Vienna, Austria, and I arrived in Austria around February 1944. In the period November to December 1944, I was assigned to digging trenches at Kittsee near Bratislava. In late December 1944, I was assigned to a work project at Zdice in Bohemia. I worked in Zdice until February 14, 1945, and when I heard that the Americans were bombing Prague, I left Zdice without permission and returned to Prague. I stayed in Prague until March 1945, and then was assigned to work in a lumber camp in the forest area of Doubravka near the city of Cerhenice, Bohemia.

In April 1945 I left this work again without permission and returned to Prague. In the early days of May 1945 there was a great deal of sporadic resistance to the Germans, and I joined a group of such resistance fighters. Our resistance activity was short-lived and did not last more than five or six days, because the Germans capitulated at this time and the war was over.

That represents a brief summary of my life during the major portion of the German occupation of Czechoslovakia.

Mr. ARENS. Would you briefly tell us now about your military career up to the time that you received training as an intelligence officer?

Mr. TISLER. As I previously mentioned, I entered the army as a draftee on October 1, 1947. My basic training lasted until November 15, 1947, at which time I was selected to attend the reserve officers' school at Klatovy. I attended this school until mid-May 1948, and while I was at this school, I was promoted to the rank of corporal in December 1947. I was subsequently promoted to sergeant in February 1948. I received field training at Boletice from May to June 1948, and then my next significant assignment was the army airborne training center at Straz pod Ralskem near Ceska Lipa. I attended another school there, and then entered the regular infantry officers' school at Hranice on October 5, 1948. I graduated from Hranice on August 17, 1949, with the rank of 2d lieutenant. I was then assigned to the regular infantry officers' school at Hranice as an instructor. It was about this time that the school moved from Hranice to Lipnik nad Becvou. While I was at the infantry school, I taught infantry tactics and supervised a platoon of students.

In March 1950 I was transferred to an airborne battalion and assumed the responsibilities of a company commander. In July 1950 I became a staff assistant to the mobilization officer of this airborne battalion. In October 1950 I was transferred to the airborne command in Prague, and I was stationed in the Ministry of National Defense building in Prague.

In October 1951 I was assigned to the Military Staff School in Prague. I attended the Faculty of General Tactics at this school, and while I was at the school I was promoted to 1st lieutenant in November 1951, and in late 1953 I was promoted to captain. After m graduation from the Military Staff School in July 1954, I requested anyassignment in Prague in operations or intelligence.

That summarizes my military career prior to the time that I became involved in intelligence activities.

Mr. ARENS. Were you ever a member of the Czechoslovak Communist Party?

Mr. TISLER. Yes, I was a member of the Czechoslovak Communist Party from April 2, 1946, until my defection in July 1959.

Mr. ARENS. Are you still an ideological believer in communism?

Mr. TISLER. No. I have not been an ideological believer in communism for a long period of time, although in the early days of my association with the Communist Party of Czechoslovakia I was an ideological believer.

Mr. ARENS. Colonel Tisler, would you outline for us briefly why you joined the Communist Party of Czechoslovakia and how it came to pass that you became disillusioned with the party?

Mr. TISLER. In October 1945 I joined the Czechoslovak National Socialist Party, and I was a member of that party until March 1946. My association with this particular political group convinced me that the policies and ideals of this party were without purpose. I was also convinced that this was a stagnant party which had no future, since this party was formed during the period of the Austro-Hungarian empire, and its original goal was the establishment of an independent Czechoslovak state. When this party was founded it was an aggressive and progressive party.

After Czechoslovakia became an independent state, the National Socialist Party lost its aggressiveness. As far as the people of my age in 1945 and 1946 were concerned, the National Socialist Party was too conservative and old-fashioned, and it did not have any real popular appeal. As a result of these factors, I resigned from the National Socialist Party. At about this same time I became interested in communism, because it appeared to me that the Communist Party of Czechoslovakia was the only Czechoslovak party which offered a bold and aggressive plan for the reconstruction of Czechoslovakia after World War II. At that time I was in many ways politically naive, and I did not appreciate the fact that the Communist Party of Czechoslovakia was, in reality, subservient to the Communist Party of the Soviet Union and, as such, was really a vehicle through which the influences of Soviet imperialism were being spread throughout Eastern Europe.

I joined the Communist Party of Czechoslovakia on April 2, 1946, and in view of my membership in the party prior to the coup of February 1948, I was considered in subsequent years to be an old ardent Communist. My initial disillusionment with communism in practice began to take place while I was attending the Military Staff School in Prague. It was at this school that I witnessed many incidents which proved to me that communism in practice was greatly different from theoretical communism.

I was exposed to numerous incidents where members of the Communist Party who were high ranking officers in the army took advantage of their position in order to obtain personal advantages and job security. It was at this time that I began to see what Djilas subsequently pointed out in his book as the development of the new class. The disillusionment which set in as a result of the excesses which were perpetrated by the so-called new class within the Communist Party began to shatter my faith in Marxism-Leninism. The doubts which I had became stronger as a result of the 1952 Slansky trials, which resulted in a blood purge within the Czechoslovak party. The subsequent rehabilitation of individuals like Rajk in Hungary and Gomulka in Poland and the lack of an admission by the Communist Party of Czechoslovakia that the Slansky trials were a fraud furthered my disillusionment. These items, plus the denigration of Stalin and the power struggle which resulted in the Soviet Union after Stalin's death, also contributed to my disillusionment.

The final factor, however, which led to my decision to break with communism was the fact that after I came to the United States in August 1955, I began to see for myself that communism as practiced in Czechoslovakia had misrepresented the true facts about the free world. The longer I stayed in the United States the better I was able to convince myself that if an individual was interested in freedom, human dignity, and life without terror, this could only be obtained in the free world. As a result I decided to remain in the United States and, as you know, I broke my ties with Czechoslovakia on July 25, 1959.

Mr. ARENS. What was the essence of the training which you received as a military intelligence officer prior to the time that you arrived in the United States?

Mr. TISLER. I was assigned to the Military Intelligence Directorate of the Czechoslovak General Staff, Ministry of National Defense, in November 1954. In December 1954 I started an intelligence training course in the vicinity of Mnichovice near Prague. This course lasted until March 1955.

Mr. ARENS. What are the responsibilities of the Military Intelligence Directorate?

Mr. TISLER. The Czechoslovak Military Intelligence Directorate is a positive intelligence service which is responsible for the overt and covert collection of information of a military nature concerning the armed forces, industrial and economic resources, and the political systems of potential enemies of Czechoslovakia.

Mr. ARENS. What type of training did you receive at the intelligence school which you attended?

Mr. TISLER. The training emphasized items such as security, the use of cover, techniques for recruiting agents in the countries of the free world, the use of secret writing, codes, and all of the other techniques which are connected with covert military intelligence operations and which we previously discussed in off-the-record sessions.

Mr. ARENS. What did you do after you completed the intelligence training course?

Mr. TISLER. After I graduated from the intelligence training course in March 1955, I returned to the headquarters of the Military Intelligence Directorate and was assigned to that headquarters component, which was responsible to intelligence operations against the United States and Great Britain. While I was connected with this unit, I also received final instructions regarding my assignment in Washington, D.C., as the military and air attaché. In the course of these preparations I was constantly reminded that my position as military and air attaché was simply a cover which was designed to legalize my presence in the United States, but my real function was that of chief of the Military Intelligence Directorate Residentura which operated from Washington, D.C., and New York against targets in the United States.

Mr. ARENS. Please elaborate on this item of "cover" and how your cover enabled you to fulfill your intelligence responsibilities.

Mr. TISLER. My cover as a military and air attaché who was accredited to the United States furnished a legal reason for my being in the United States and being assigned to the Czechoslovak Embassy in Washington, D.C. This legal reason enabled me to meet and develop contacts with other foreign diplomats who were accredited to the United States. It also provided me with a valid reason for being interested in military developments in the United States. In this cover position I was to interest myself in United States military matters, but at the same time these cover duties were not to detract from my real mission. This mission called for me to attempt to personally recruit American citizens to act as agents and, in their agent capacities, to furnish me with intelligence on classified materials related to United States military developments. The officers of my staff were also engaged in similar operations, although not all of them used the cover of the military attaché's office. As the military and air attaché I had office facilities in the Czechoslovak Embassy in Washington, D.C., and these office facilities were used to house my records and equipment, which I used for clandestine intelligence purposes. This means that the Czechoslovak Embassy was used to house an intelligence residentura, which was engaged in activities which were inimical to the best interests of the United States Government. The precise nature and details of these activities, as you know, we have discussed extensively in off-the-record sessions.

Mr. ARENS. Now, was the Czechoslovak ambassador to the United States aware of your responsibilities as an intelligence officer?

Mr. TISLER. Yes. The ambassador was aware of the fact that I was the chief of the Military Intelligence Directorate Residentura in the United States and that I and members of my staff were engaged in covert clandestine activity against the United States.

Mr. ARENS. Did the ambassador try to interfere or restrain you from conducting these activities?

Mr. TISLER. I was accredited to the United States during the period August 30, 1955 to July 25, 1959, and in this period of time the Czech ambassadors to the United States were Petrzelka and Ruzek, the present ambassador. Although both of these ambassadors were aware of my intelligence functions, they did not in any way interfere with my activities nor did they attempt to restrain me from engaging in such activities.

Mr. ARENS. Off the record.

(Discussion off the record.)

Mr. ARENS. Colonel Tisler, were the activities which you and the members of your residentura conducted the only intelligence activities which were operated from the Czechoslovak Embassy in Washington, D.C.?

Mr. TISLER. No.

Mr. ARENS. Would you elaborate on this point?

Mr. TISLER. I can only say that the Czechoslovak Ministry of Interior also had a residentura in the embassy in Washington, D.C., and a sub-office in New York. The chief of this residentura was also known to the Czechoslovak ambassador, and this residentura was responsible for the covert and overt collection of political, scientific, and economic intelligence on potential enemies of Czechoslovakia. As Czechoslovakia regards the United States as one of its potential enemies, the Ministry of Interior Residentura was also engaged in covert clandestine activities against the best .interests of the United States. As far as I know, the Czechoslovak ambassador to the United States did not attempt to restrain or hinder the activities of this residentura.

· Mr. ARENS. Would you indicate to us the number of officers who were on your staff and who were active in military intelligence activities against the United States? In so doing, it would be appreciated if you could also make some comment as to the types of cover that were used by the members of your staff. It is understood, of course, that certain incidents and names are not to be revealed in this session here, as the information from this session will eventually be made public.

Mr. TISLER. The Military Intelligence Residentura in the United States during the period August 1955 to July 1959 generally consisted of five officers. Four officers were assigned to the Czechoslovak Embassy in Washington, D.C., and one officer was assigned to the permanent Czechoslovak delegation to the United Nations. I was responsible for supervising the activities of all of these officers. Of this total number, two officers used the cover of the military attaché's office, whereas one officer used the cover of the commercial attaché's section of the Czechoslovak Embassy, and two officers used the cover of the Ministry of Foreign Affairs.

· Mr. ARENS. Are we to deduce from your remarks regarding the cover which was employed by the members of your residentura that similar cover mechanisms were used by officers of the residentura of the Ministry of Interior?

Mr. TISLER. Yes, that would be an accurate deduction, although Ministry of Interior personnel tend to use the cover of the Ministry of Foreign Affairs to a greater extent than does the Military Intelligence Directorate.

Mr. ARENS. Could you tell us the number of Ministry of Interior intelligence officers who were operating in the United States during the period August 1955 to July 1959?

Mr. TISLER. As you know, we have discussed this in off-the-record sessions. As a result, I believe that it would be sufficient to say at this session that during the period from August 1955 to July 1959 approximately 45 percent of the personnel at the Czechoslovak Embassy in Washington, D.C., and of the Czechoslovak delegation to the United Nations in New York was engaged in some type of intelligence activity while in this country.

Mr. ARENS. Would it be accurate to say that we can deduce from this figure that one of the main reasons for the maintenance of a Czechoslovak Embassy in Washington, D.C., is to conduct espionage against the United States?

Mr. TISLER. Yes, that would be an accurate deduction, as it is based on fact.

Mr. ARENS. Colonel Tisler, are you aware of any American citizens or nationals who were in contact with members of either the Czechoslovak Embassy in Washington, D.C., or members of the Czechoslovak delegation to the United Nations in New York who were, or appeared to be, working for Czechoslovakia against the best interests of the United States?

Mr. TISLER. I know that members of the Czechoslovak Embassy in Washington, D.C., were in frequent contact with Antonin Krchmarek and Charles Musil.

Mr. ARENS. Would you outline to us the nature of Krchmarek's relationship with members of the staff of the Czechoslovak Embassy in Washington, D.C.?

Mr. TISLER. I know that Antonin Krchmarek is an American of Czech origin who apparently resides in Cleveland, Ohio. This Krchmarek was involved in a Smith Act trial of leading members of the Communist Party of the United States. As far as I know, Krchmarek was arrested at some point in 1953, and during the course of his trial regarding violations of the Smith Act, the Czechoslovak Government was very concerned about Krchmarek's case. In order to assist Krchmarek in this trial, funds were transferred from members of the embasssy staff to intermediaries, who subsequently saw to it that these funds were used to aid Krchmarek in his defense during the trial for alleged violations of the Smith Act.

In 1956 the Czechoslovak Government was interested in inviting several United States public officials of Czechoslovak descent to visit Czechoslovakia. As a result, the Czechoslovak Embassy in Washington, D.C., was requested to submit a list of names of such officials, as well as personality data on these individuals. As far as I can recall, somewhere around May 1956, Ambassador Petrzelka advised the Ministry of Foreign Affairs that, in view of the fact that 1956 was an election year, it would be difficult to arrange visits of public officials to Czechoslovakia. Ambassador Petrzelka suggested that perhaps rather than invite public officials, Czechoslovakia should concentrate on arranging the travel of scientific, economic, or cultural experts to Czechoslovakia. It was at approximately this time that members of the embassy staff in Washington, D.C., contacted Antonin Krchmarek in order to determine whether he knew certain public figures who might be invited to visit Czechoslovakia. As far as I can recall, Krchmarek advised the embassy that certain individuals whom he designated should be invited to visit Czechoslovakia, but invitations should not be given to certain other named persons.

Mr. ARENS. Are you aware of any other reports which Krchmarek may have submitted to the Czechoslovak Embassy in Washington, D.C.?

Mr. TISLER. I recall that in December 1958 Ambassador Petrzelka sent a report to the Ministry of Foreign Affairs in Prague about the 4 November 1958 elections in the United States. This report contained an analysis of the election, and attached to this report were notes from Krchmarek regarding these elections. As a result I assume that Krchmarek must have presented some analytical comments on these elections to members of the embassy staff.

Mr. ARENS. Do you know anything about Krchmarek's travels to Czechoslovakia in 1950?

Mr. TISLER. I have heard that Krchmarek was in Prague for a year or so in the period around 1950. While in Prague, Krchmarek was associated with the Czechoslovak Foreign Institute. On the other hand, I must remind you that I did not personally see Krchmarek in Czechoslovakia.

Mr. ARENS. Would you tell us what you know about the Czechoslovak Foreign Institute?

Mr. TISLER. The Czechoslovak Foreign Institute is located in Prague, and it is responsible for taking care of Czechs and Slovaks who are abroad. This institute publishes the magazine *Czechoslovak World* (*Ceskoslovensky Svet*). As a result, it is clear that the real purpose of this institute is the overt spreading of Czechoslovak propaganda and the exercise of covert Czechoslovak Communist Party control over the Czech and Slovak minorities abroad.

Mr. ARENS. Was Krchmarek's association with the Czechoslovak Foreign Institute one of the reasons why the Czechoslovak Government was so interested in keeping abreast of all developments regarding Krchmarek's indictment for violation of the Smith Act?

Mr. TISLER. I am certain that the Czechoslovak Government did not want any information to appear in the American press regarding Krchmarek's association with the Czechoslovak Foreign Institute, as this could have been interpreted by American authorities as an indication that Krchmarek was either a political action agent of Czechoslovakia or that Czechoslovakia was using Krchmarek as a means of interfering in the internal affairs of the United States.

Mr. ARENS. Do you know if Krchmarek was an agent of the Czechoslovak Government?

Mr. TISLER. Krchmarek met various members of the embassy staff on various occasions and furnished them with information on a wide variety of topics. As an example, Krchmarek met Ambassador Petrzelka in New York during August 1958, and at this meeting Krchmarek told Petrzelka that Krchmarek had recently been made a member of the Executive Committee of the Central Committee of the Communist Party of the United States of America. At this meeting Krchmarek informed Petrzelka as to the trends and developments which were taking place within the Communist Party of the United States of America. This information was subsequently relayed by Petrzelka to the International Section of the Central Committee of the Communist Party of Czechoslovakia.

Mr. ARENS. Are you aware of any incidents or occasions in which Krchmarek received funds from the Czechoslovak Government?

Mr. TISLER. I mentioned earlier that the Czechoslovak Government made contributions to Krchmarek's defense fund at the time that Krchmarek was on trial for violations of the Smith Act. I am also aware of the fact that Krchmarek had requested that Ambassador Petrzelka obtain financial support from the Communist Party of Czechoslovakia for the activities of the Communist Party of the United States. At the same time, I know that Ambassador Petrzelka has paid Krchmarek funds to cover travel expenses involved in Krchmarek meeting Ambassador Petrzelka in New York. In January 1956 Petrzelka advised Prague that Krchmarek was without funds, and it was Ambassador Petrzelka's recommendation that he be authorized to pay Krchmarek $3,000 for living expenses and propaganda activities.

Mr. ARENS. Who in Czechoslovakia directed Krchmarek's activities in the United States?

Mr. TISLER. The correspondence relating to Krchmarek was either sent to the Czechoslovak Foreign Institute, the Ministry of Foreign Affairs, or the International Section of the Central Committee of the Communist Party of Czechoslovakia. It is my opinion that the direction of Krchmarek's activities in the United States was furnished by the International Section of the Central Committee of the Communist Party of Czechoslovakia. This opinion is based to a large extent upon the fact that information was sent to Krchmarek from the International Section of the Central Committee of the Communist

Party of Czechoslovakia, and this material was relayed to Krchmarek via the good offices of the embassy staff.

Mr. ARENS. What can you tell us about the relationship between the Czechoslovak Embassy in Washington, D.C., and Charles Musil?

Mr. TISLER. I know that Charles Musil was, or even still may be, the editor of a Czech-language newspaper which is published in Chicago, Illinois, under the title, *Nova Doba.* In December 1955 the Czechoslovak Ministry of Foreign Affairs requested that the Czech Embassy in Washington, D.C., offer advice as to whether the Czechoslovak Foreign Institute should establish direct contact with Musil in order that this institute could send Musil propaganda material which they wanted to appear in *Nova Doba.* I don't know what the results of this correspondence were, but I am aware of the fact that the *Nova Doba* newspaper is Communist-dominated and generally follows the line of the international Communist movement. I also recall that in November 1956 the Czechoslovak Embassy in Washington, D.C., advised the Ministry of Foreign Affairs in Prague that Musil had been accused by United States authorities as being a member of the Communist Party of the United States.

Mr. ARENS. Are you aware of any other activities which Musil conducted on behalf of the Czechoslovak Embassy or the Czechoslovak Government?

Mr. TISLER. In January 1956 Musil had several meetings with Ambassador Petrzelka and, during the course of these meetings, furnished the ambassador with information related to Krchmarek's status and difficulties. In this period Ambassador Petrzelka used Musil as an intermediary between himself and Krchmarek. The use of Musil as an intermediary seems to have its origins in the fact that, when Ambassador Petrzelka talked to Soviet Ambassador Zarubin in January and February 1954 regarding Ambassador Petrzelka's contacts with Krchmarek and the Communist Party of the United States, Soviet Ambassador Zarubin recommended that in view of the likely harmful repercussions which could develop if the Krchmarek trial revealed that Krchmarek was in direct contact with members of the Czechoslovak Embassy, it was recommended that this contact be handled via intermediaries. In this connection Zarubin told Ambassador Petrzelka that the Soviets never maintained direct contact with members of the Communist Party of the United States, because the Soviets wanted to avoid any embarrassment.

Mr. ARENS. Colonel, this session has been extremely helpful, as have our other, off-the-record sessions. I assume that there is no objection on your part to our ultimately making today's session a matter of public record.

Mr. TISLER. In view of the fact that we have been careful to see that the material which we discussed today will not result in any harm coming to innocent people who are still behind the Iron Curtain, I do not have any objections to today's session being made a matter of public record.

The CHAIRMAN. Colonel Tisler, I want to take this opportunity to thank you for your excellent cooperation. At the same time, I want to assure you, on behalf of the United States Government, that we will render all possible assistance in helping you to build a new life for yourself in the United States which will give you the freedom that you want.

INDEX

INDIVIDUALS

ORGANIZATIONS

PUBLICATIONS

i

CPSIA information can be obtained
at www.ICGtesting.com
Printed in the USA
LVOW13*2158060818
586121LV00010B/258/P